THE COMMON CORE

Clarifying Expectations for Teachers & Students

ENGLISH LANGUAGE ARTS

Grade 1

Created and Presented by
Align, Assess, Achieve

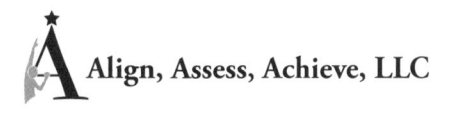

Mc Graw Hill Education

Align, Assess, Achieve, LLC

STEM McGraw-Hill is committed to providing instructional materials in Science, Technology, Engineering, and Mathematics (STEM) that give all students a solid foundation, one that prepares them for college and careers in the 21st century.

Send all inquiries to:
McGraw-Hill Education
STEM Learning Solutions Center
8787 Orion Place
Columbus, OH 43240

ISBN: 978-002-123279-6
MHID: 0-02-123279-2

Printed in the United States of America.

2 3 4 5 6 7 8 9 QLM 16 15 14 13 12

Our mission is to provide educational resources that enable students to become the problem solvers of the 21st century and inspire them to explore careers within Science, Technology, Engineering, and Mathematics (STEM) related fields.

Acknowledgements

This book integrates the Common Core State Standards – a framework for educating students to be competitive at an international level – with well-researched instructional planning strategies for achieving the goals of the CCSS. Our work is rooted in the thinking of brilliant educators, such as Grant Wiggins, Jay McTighe, and Rick Stiggins, and enriched by our work with a great number of inspiring teachers, administrators, and parents. We hope this book provides a meaningful contribution to the ongoing conversation around educating lifelong, passionate learners.

We would like to thank many talented contributors who helped create *The Common Core: Clarifying Expectations for Teachers and Students.* Our authors, Lani Meyers and Mindy Holmes, for their intelligence, persistence, and love of teaching; Graphic Designer Thomas Davis, for his creative talents and good nature through many trials; Editors, Laura Gage and Dr. Teresa Dempsey, for their educational insights and encouragement; Director of book editing and production Josh Steskal, for his feedback, organization, and unwavering patience; Our spouses, Andrew Bainbridge and Tawnya Holman, who believe in our mission and have, through their unconditional support and love, encouraged us to take risks and grow.

Katy Bainbridge
Bob Holman
Co-Founders
Align, Assess, Achieve, LLC

Executive Editors: *Katy Bainbridge and Bob Holman*
Authors: *Mindy Holmes and Lani Meyers*
Contributing Authors: *Teresa Dempsey, Katy Bainbridge and Bob Holman*
Graphic Design & Layout: *Thomas Davis; thomasanceldesign.com*
Director of Book Editing & Production: *Josh Steskal*

Introduction

Purpose

The Common Core State Standards (CCSS) provide educators across the nation with a shared vision for student achievement. They also provide a shared challenge: how to interpret the standards and use them in a meaningful way? Clarifying the Common Core was designed to facilitate the transition to the CCSS at the district, building, and classroom level.

Organization

Clarifying the Common Core presents content from two sources: the CCSS and Align, Assess, Achieve. Content from the CCSS is located in the top section of each page and includes the strand, CCR, and grade level standard. The second section of each page contains content created by Align, Assess, Achieve – Enduring Understandings, Essential Questions, Suggested Learning Targets, and Vocabulary. The black bar at the bottom of the page contains the CCSS standard identifier. A sample page can be found in the next section.

Planning for Instruction and Assessment

This book was created to foster meaningful instruction of the CCSS. This requires planning both quality instruction and assessment. Designing and using quality assessments is key to high-quality instruction (Stiggins et al.). Assessment should accurately measure the intended learning and should inform further instruction. This is only possible when teachers and students have a clear vision of the intended learning. When planning instruction it helps to ask two questions, "Where am I taking my students?" and "How will we get there?" The first question refers to the big picture and is addressed with **Enduring Understandings** and **Essential Questions**. The second question points to the instructional process and is addressed by **Learning Targets**.

Where Am I Taking My Students?

When planning, it is useful to think about the larger, lasting instructional concepts as **Enduring Understandings**. Enduring Understandings are rooted in multiple units of instruction throughout the year and are often utilized K-12. These concepts represent the lasting understandings that transcend your content. Enduring Understandings serve as the ultimate goal of a teacher's instructional planning. Although tempting to share with students initially, we do not recommend telling students the Enduring Understanding in advance. Rather, Enduring Understandings are developed through meaningful engagement with an Essential Question.

Essential Questions work in concert with Enduring Understandings to ignite student curiosity. These questions help students delve deeper and make connections between the concepts and the content they are learning. Essential Questions are designed with the student in mind and do not have an easy answer; rather, they are used to spark inquiry into the deeper meanings (Wiggins and McTighe). Therefore, we advocate frequent use of Essential Questions with students. It is sometimes helpful to think of the Enduring Understanding as the answer to the Essential Question.

How Will We Get There?

If Enduring Understandings and Essential Questions represent the larger, conceptual ideas, then what guides the learning of specific knowledge, reasoning, and skills? These are achieved by using **Learning Targets**. Learning Targets represent a logical, student friendly progression of teaching and learning. Targets are the scaffolding students climb as they progress towards deeper meaning.

There are four types of learning targets, based on what students are asked to do: knowledge, reasoning/understanding, skill, and product (Stiggins et al.). When selecting Learning Targets, teachers need to ask, "What is the goal of instruction?" After answering this question, select the target or targets that align to the instructional goal.

Instructional Goal	*Target Type*	*Key Verbs*
Recall basic information and facts	Knowledge (K)	Name, identify, describe
Think and develop an understanding	Reasoning/ Understanding (R)	Explain, compare and contrast, predict
Apply knowledge and reasoning	Skill (S)	Use, solve, calculate
Synthesize to create original work	Product (P)	Create, write, present

Adapted from Stiggins et al. *Classroom Assessment for Student Learning.* (Portland: ETS, 2006). Print.

Keep in mind that the Enduring Understandings, Essential Questions, and Learning Targets in this book are suggestions. Modify and combine the content as necessary to meet your instructional needs. Quality instruction consists of clear expectations, ongoing assessment, and effective feedback. Taken together, these promote meaningful instruction that facilitates student mastery of the Common Core State Standards.

References

Stiggins, Rick, Jan Chappuis, Judy Arter, and Steve Chappuis. *Classroom Assessment for Student Learning.* 2nd. Portland, OR: ETS, 2006.

Wiggins, Grant, and Jay McTighe. *Understanding by Design, Expanded 2nd Edition.* 2nd. Alexandria, VA: ASCD, 2005.

Page Organization

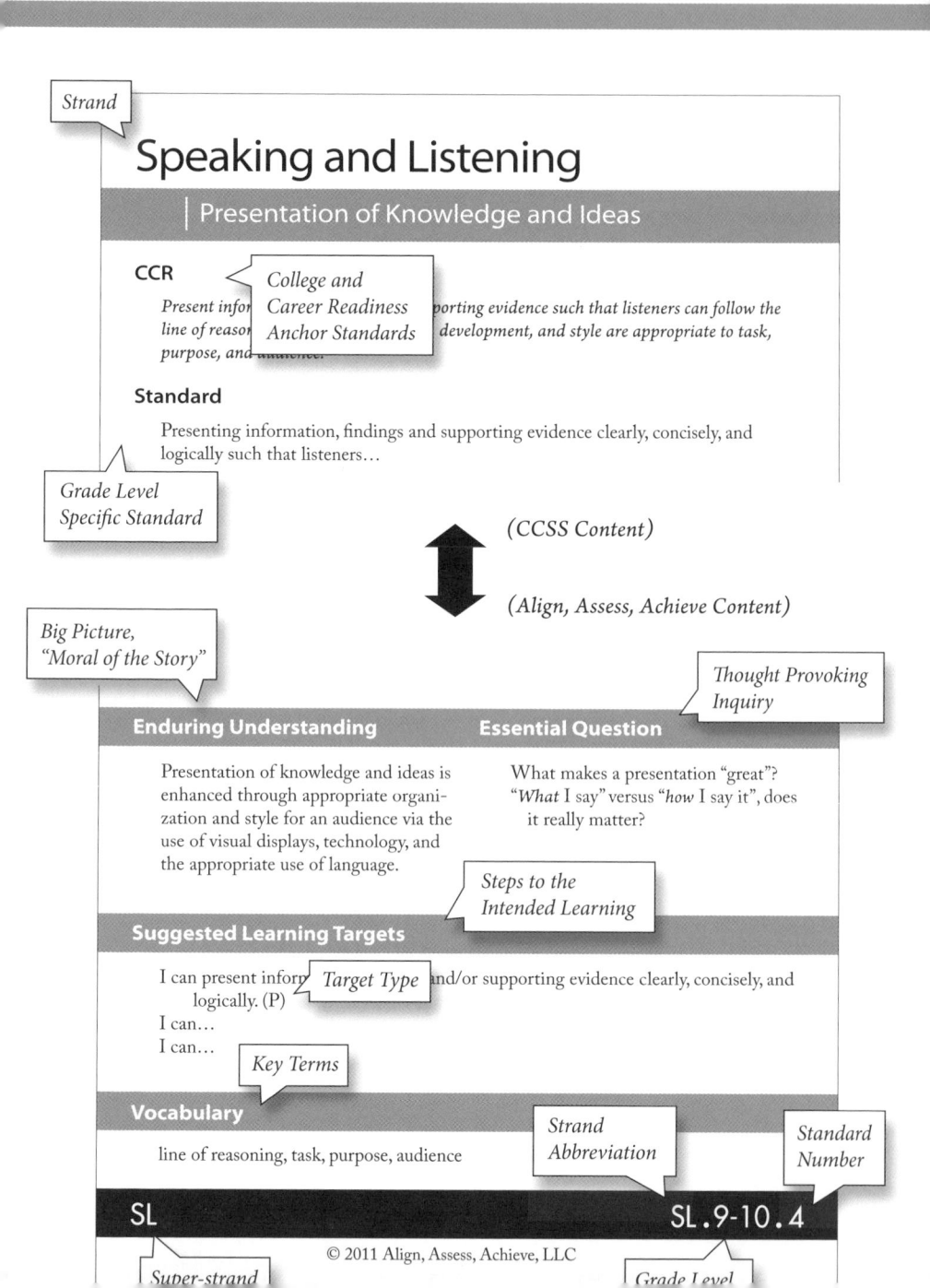

Strand

Speaking and Listening

| Presentation of Knowledge and Ideas

CCR

College and Career Readiness Anchor Standards

Present infor   porting evidence such that listeners can follow the line of reason   development, and style are appropriate to task, purpose, and

Standard

Presenting information, findings and supporting evidence clearly, concisely, and logically such that listeners…

Grade Level Specific Standard

(CCSS Content)

(Align, Assess, Achieve Content)

Big Picture, "Moral of the Story"

Thought Provoking Inquiry

Enduring Understanding	**Essential Question**
Presentation of knowledge and ideas is enhanced through appropriate organization and style for an audience via the use of visual displays, technology, and the appropriate use of language.	What makes a presentation "great"? "*What* I say" versus "*how* I say it", does it really matter?

Steps to the Intended Learning

Suggested Learning Targets

I can present infor *Target Type* nd/or supporting evidence clearly, concisely, and logically. (P)
I can…
I can…

Key Terms

Vocabulary

line of reasoning, task, purpose, audience

Strand Abbreviation

Standard Number

SL

SL.9-10.4

Super-strand

Grade Level

Literature

CCR

Read closely to determine what the text says explicitly and to make logical inferences from it; cite specific textual evidence when writing or speaking to support conclusions drawn from the text.

Standard

Ask and answer questions about key details in a text.

Enduring Understanding

Effective readers use a variety of strategies to make sense of key ideas and details presented in text.

Essential Questions

What do good readers do?
Am I clear about what I just read?
How do I know?

Suggested Learning Targets

I can explain that a key detail is an important part of a text. (K)
I can identify key details in a text (e.g., *who*, *what*, *where*, *when*, *why*, and *how*). (S)
I can ask and answer questions about key details in a text. (S)

Vocabulary

key detail

R   RL.1.1

Literature

CCR

Determine central ideas or themes of a text and analyze their development; summarize the key supporting details and ideas.

Standard

Retell stories, including key details, and demonstrate understanding of their central message or lesson.

Enduring Understanding

Effective readers use a variety of strategies to make sense of key ideas and details presented in text.

Essential Questions

What do good readers do?
Am I clear about what I just read?
How do I know?

Suggested Learning Targets

I can retell (put into my own words) stories using key details. (S)
I can define central message or lesson (the overall idea an author is trying to share). (K)
I can determine the central message or lesson found in a story using key details. (S)

Vocabulary

retell, key detail, central message, lesson

Literature

CCR

Analyze how and why individuals, events, and ideas develop and interact over the course of a text.

Standard

Describe characters, settings, and major events in a story, using key details.

Enduring Understanding

Effective readers use a variety of strategies to make sense of key ideas and details presented in text.

Essential Questions

What do good readers do?
Am I clear about what I just read?
How do I know?

Suggested Learning Targets

I can identify the characters, settings, and major events in a story. (K)
I can use key details to describe the characters in a story. (S)
I can use key details to describe the settings in a story. (S)
I can use key details to describe the major events in a story. (S)

Vocabulary

character, setting, major event, key detail

R

RL.1.3

Literature

CCR

Interpret words and phrases as they are used in a text, including determining technical, connotative, and figurative meanings, and analyze how specific word choices shape meaning or tone.

Standard

Identify words and phrases in stories or poems that suggest feelings or appeal to the senses.

Enduring Understanding

Analyzing texts for structure, purpose, and viewpoint allows an effective reader to gain insight and strengthen understanding.

Essential Questions

Author's choice: Why does it matter? What makes a story a "great" story?

Suggested Learning Targets

I can identify the five senses (sight, hearing, taste, touch, smell). (K)
I can identify words and phrases in a story or poem that tell me how something looks, sounds, tastes, feels, or smells. (S)

Vocabulary

five senses

Literature

CCR

Analyze the structure of texts, including how specific sentences, paragraphs, and larger portions of the text (e.g., a section, chapter, scene, or stanza) relate to each other and the whole.

Standard

Explain major differences between books that tell stories and books that give information, drawing on a wide reading of a range of text types.

Enduring Understanding

Analyzing texts for structure, purpose, and viewpoint allows an effective reader to gain insight and strengthen understanding.

Essential Questions

Author's choice: Why does it matter? What makes a story a "great" story?

Suggested Learning Targets

I can read or listen to books that tell stories. (S)
I can read or listen to books that give information. (S)
I can explain the differences between books that tell stories and books that give information. (R)

Vocabulary

story, information

R

RL.1.5

Literature

CCR

Assess how point of view or purpose shapes the content and style of a text.

Standard

Identify who is telling the story at various points in a text.

Enduring Understanding

Analyzing texts for structure, purpose, and viewpoint allows an effective reader to gain insight and strengthen understanding.

Essential Questions

Author's choice: Why does it matter? What makes a story a "great" story?

Suggested Learning Targets

I can identify the characters in a story. (K)
I can recognize when more than one character is telling the story. (R)
I can identify when the character telling the story changes. (S)
I can identify the character telling the story at any point. (S)

Vocabulary

character

Literature

CCR

Integrate and evaluate content presented in diverse media and formats, including visually and quantitatively, as well as in words.*

Standard

Use illustrations and details in a story to describe its characters, setting, or events.

*Please see "Research to Build and Present Knowledge" in Writing and "Comprehension and Collaboration" in Speaking and Listening for additional standards relevant to gathering, assessing, and applying information from print and digital sources.

Enduring Understanding

To gain keener insight into the integration of knowledge and ideas, effective readers analyze and evaluate content, reasoning, and claims in diverse formats.

Essential Questions

In what ways does creative choice impact an audience?
Whose story is it, and why does it matter?

Suggested Learning Targets

I can look at the illustrations in a story and describe what I see. (K)
I can identify details in a story that tell me about the characters, setting, or events. (K)
I can describe the characters, setting, or events of a story using illustrations and details. (S)

Vocabulary

illustration, detail, character, setting, event

R

RL.1.7

Literature

CCR

Delineate and evaluate the argument and specific claims in a text, including the validity of the reasoning as well as the relevance and sufficiency of the evidence.

Standard

(Not applicable to literature)

(No Common Core State Standard #8 for Reading and Literature)

Literature

CCR

Analyze how two or more texts address similar themes or topics in order to build knowledge or to compare the approaches the authors take.

Standard

Compare and contrast the adventures and experiences of characters in stories.

Enduring Understanding

To gain keener insight into the integration of knowledge and ideas, effective readers analyze and evaluate content, reasoning, and claims in diverse formats.

Essential Questions

In what ways does creative choice impact an audience?
Whose story is it, and why does it matter?

Suggested Learning Targets

I can identify characters in stories I read or hear. (K)
I can describe the adventures and experiences of characters in stories I read or hear. (K)
I can compare the adventures and experiences of characters by telling how they are alike. (R)
I can contrast the adventures and experiences of characters by telling how they are different. (R)

Vocabulary

character, adventure, experience, compare, contrast

R

RL.1.9

Literature

CCR

Read and comprehend complex literary and informational texts independently and proficiently.

Standard

With prompting and support, read prose and poetry of appropriate complexity for grade 1.

Enduring Understanding

Effective readers use a variety of strategies to make sense of the ideas and details presented in text.

Essential Questions

What do good readers do?
Am I clear about what I just read?
How do I know?

Suggested Learning Targets

I can read first grade sight words (high-frequency words). (S)
I can read short books and poems and ask for help when needed. (S)

Vocabulary

sight word

R   RL.1.10

Informational Text

CCR

Read closely to determine what the text says explicitly and to make logical inferences from it; cite specific textual evidence when writing or speaking to support conclusions drawn from the text.

Standard

Ask and answer questions about key details in a text.

Enduring Understanding

Effective readers use a variety of strategies to make sense of key ideas and details presented in text.

Essential Questions

What do good readers do?
Am I clear about what I just read?
How do I know?

Suggested Learning Targets

I can explain that a key detail is an important part of a text. (K)
I can identify key details in a text (e.g., *who, what, where, when, why*, and *how*). (S)
I can ask and answer questions about key details in a text. (S)

Vocabulary

key detail

R

RI.1.1

Informational Text

CCR

Determine central ideas or themes of a text and analyze their development; summarize the key supporting details and ideas.

Standard

Identify the main topic and retell key details of a text.

Enduring Understanding

Effective readers use a variety of strategies to make sense of key ideas and details presented in text.

Essential Questions

What do good readers do?
Am I clear about what I just read?
How do I know?

Suggested Learning Targets

I can define main idea/topic (who or what the text is mostly about). (K)
I can identify the main idea or topic of a text. (S)
I can retell the key details of a text (e.g., *who, what, where, when, why,* and *how*). (S)

Vocabulary

main idea, topic, retell, key detail

Informational Text

CCR

Analyze how and why individuals, events, and ideas develop and interact over the course of a text.

Standard

Describe the connection between two individuals, events, ideas, or pieces of information in a text.

Enduring Understanding

Effective readers use a variety of strategies to make sense of key ideas and details presented in text.

Essential Questions

What do good readers do?
Am I clear about what I just read?
How do I know?

Suggested Learning Targets

I can identify individuals, events, ideas, or pieces of information in a text. (K)
I can describe a connection between two individuals in a text (e.g., *Clifford is Emily Elizabeth's dog.*). (R)
I can describe a connection between two events in a text (e.g., *The Pilgrims come to America; the first Thanksgiving is celebrated.*). (R)
I can describe a connection between two ideas or pieces of information in a text (e.g., *The sun and moon are both in the sky.*). (R)

Vocabulary

individual, event, idea/piece of information, connection

R

RI.1.3

Informational Text

CCR

Interpret words and phrases as they are used in a text, including determining technical, connotative, and figurative meanings, and analyze how specific word choices shape meaning or tone.

Standard

Ask and answer questions to help determine or clarify the meaning of words and phrases in a text.

Enduring Understanding

Analyzing texts for structure, purpose, and viewpoint allows an effective reader to gain insight and strengthen understanding.

Essential Questions

Author's choice: Why does it matter? What makes a story a "great" story?

Suggested Learning Targets

I can identify unknown or unclear words and phrases. (K)
I can clarify or learn the meaning of words and phrases by asking and answering questions. (S)

Vocabulary

clarify, phrase

R   RI.1.4

Informational Text

Craft and Structure

CCR

Analyze the structure of texts, including how specific sentences, paragraphs, and larger portions of the text (e.g., a section, chapter, scene, or stanza) relate to each other and the whole.

Standard

Know and use various text features (e.g., headings, tables of contents, glossaries, electronic menus, icons) to locate key facts or information in a text.

Enduring Understanding

Analyzing texts for structure, purpose, and viewpoint allows an effective reader to gain insight and strengthen understanding.

Essential Questions

Author's choice: Why does it matter? What makes a story a "great" story?

Suggested Learning Targets

I can identify and give examples of text features. (K)
I can explain how text features help locate key facts or information. (R)
I can locate key facts or information using text features. (S)

Vocabulary

text feature, key fact, information

R   RI.1.5

Informational Text

| Craft and Structure

CCR

Assess how point of view or purpose shapes the content and style of a text.

Standard

Distinguish between information provided by pictures or other illustrations and information provided by the words in a text.

Enduring Understanding

Analyzing texts for structure, purpose, and viewpoint allows an effective reader to gain insight and strengthen understanding.

Essential Questions

Author's choice: Why does it matter? What makes a story a "great" story?

Suggested Learning Targets

I can locate pictures and illustrations in a text. (K)
I can explain what I learn from looking at a picture or illustration in a text. (R)
I can explain what I learn from reading or hearing the words of a text. (R)
I can tell the difference between what I learned from pictures or illustrations and
    what I learned from words. (S)

Vocabulary

picture, illustration, difference

R

RI.1.6

Informational Text

CCR

Integrate and evaluate content presented in diverse media and formats, including visually and quantitatively, as well as in words.*

Standard

Use the illustrations and details in a text to describe its key ideas.

*Please see "Research to Build and Present Knowledge" in Writing and "Comprehension and Collaboration" in Speaking and Listening for additional standards relevant to gathering, assessing, and applying information from print and digital sources.

Enduring Understanding

To gain keener insight into the integration of knowledge and ideas, effective readers analyze and evaluate content, reasoning, and claims in diverse formats.

Essential Questions

In what ways does creative choice impact an audience?
Whose story is it, and why does it matter?

Suggested Learning Targets

I can describe an illustration in a text. (S)
I can identify details in a text. (S)
I can use the illustrations and details in a text to describe the key ideas. (S)

Vocabulary

key idea, detail, illustration

R   RI . 1 . 7

Informational Text

CCR

Delineate and evaluate the argument and specific claims in a text, including the validity of the reasoning as well as the relevance and sufficiency of the evidence.

Standard

Identify the reasons an author gives to support points in a text.

Enduring Understanding

To gain keener insight into the integration of knowledge and ideas, effective readers analyze and evaluate content, reasoning, and claims in diverse formats.

Essential Questions

In what ways does creative choice impact an audience?
Whose story is it, and why does it matter?

Suggested Learning Targets

I can identify why an author wrote a text. (K)
I can identify the points an author makes in a text (e.g., *Everyone should recycle.*). (K)
I can identify the reasons an author gives to support the points in a text (e.g., *Everyone should recycle because landfills are becoming full.*). (R)

Vocabulary

point, reason

R   RI.1.8

Informational Text

CCR

Analyze how two or more texts address similar themes or topics in order to build knowledge or to compare the approaches the authors take.

Standard

Identify basic similarities in and differences between two texts on the same topic (e.g., in illustrations, descriptions, or procedures).

Enduring Understanding

To gain keener insight into the integration of knowledge and ideas, effective readers analyze and evaluate content, reasoning, and claims in diverse formats.

Essential Questions

In what ways does creative choice impact an audience?
Whose story is it, and why does it matter?

Suggested Learning Targets

I can compare two texts on the same topic by telling how they are alike. (R)
I can contrast two texts on the same topic by telling how they are different. (R)

Vocabulary

compare, contrast

R   RI.1.9

Informational Text

CCR

Read and comprehend complex literary and informational texts independently and proficiently.

Standard

With prompting and support, read informational texts appropriately complex for grade 1.

Enduring Understanding

Effective readers use a variety of strategies to make sense of the ideas and details presented in text.

Essential Questions

What do good readers do?
Am I clear about what I just read?
How do I know?

Suggested Learning Targets

I can identify and read sight words (high-frequency words). (S)
I can read short informational texts and ask for help when needed. (S)

Vocabulary

sight word, informational text

R

RI.1.10

Foundational Skills

CCR

(Not applicable to Foundational Skills)

Standard

Demonstrate understanding of the organization and basic features of print.

a. Recognize the distinguishing features of a sentence (e.g., first word, capitalization, ending punctuation).

Enduring Understanding

Foundational elements of literacy require a working knowledge of the organization and basic features of print.

Essential Questions

What do good readers do?
What do good writers do?

Suggested Learning Targets

I can identify letters, words, and sentences. (K)
I can recognize that words are combined to make sentence. (K)
I can recognize that the first word in a sentence is capitalized. (K)
I can recognize that words are separated by spaces before and after them. (K)
I can recognize that a sentence ends with a punctuation mark (e.g., period, question mark, exclamation point). (K)

Vocabulary

letter, word, sentence, capitalize, punctuation mark

R
RF.1.1

Foundational Skills

CCR

(Not applicable to Foundational Skills)

Standard

Demonstrate understanding of spoken words, syllables, and sounds (phonemes).

a. Distinguish long from short vowel sounds in spoken single-syllable words.
b. Orally produce single-syllable words by blending sounds (phonemes), including consonant blends.
c. Isolate and pronounce initial, medial vowel, and final sounds (phonemes) in spoken single-syllable words.
d. Segment spoken single-syllable words into their complete sequence of individual sounds (phonemes).

Enduring Understanding

Recognizing the relationship between sounds, syllables, and spoken words is foundational for future success as a reader.

Essential Questions

Why are sounds and letters important? How do sounds and letters create words?

Suggested Learning Targets

I can identify short vowel sounds in single-syllable words (e.g., *cat*, *sit*, *hop*). (K)
I can identify long vowel sounds in single-syllable words (e.g., *bake*, *mine*, *hope*). (K)
I can tell the difference between long and short vowel sounds. (R)
I can identify the sound each letter makes. (K)
I can recognize that blending letters can create new sounds. (K)
I can sound out words by blending letter sounds. (S)
I break words into beginning, middle, and ending sound segments. (S)

Vocabulary

short vowel, long vowel, syllable, letter, blend, segment

R

RF.1.2

Foundational Skills

CCR

(Not applicable to Foundational Skills)

Standard

Know and apply grade-level phonics and word analysis skills in decoding words.

a. Know the spelling-sound correspondences for common consonant digraphs (two letters that represent one sound).
b. Decode regularly spelled one-syllable words.
c. Know final -e and common vowel team conventions for representing long vowel sounds.
d. Use knowledge that every syllable must have a vowel sound to determine the number of syllables in a printed word.
e. Decode two-syllable words following basic patterns by breaking the words into syllables.
f. Read words with inflectional endings.
g. Recognize and read grade-appropriate irregularly spelled words.

Enduring Understanding

Word analysis and decoding skills are foundational for success as a reader.

Essential Questions

How do sounds and letters create words? When a word doesn't make sense, what can I do?

Suggested Learning Targets

I can identify the sounds each letter makes. (K)
I can identify and create the sounds common digraphs make (e.g., *sh, ph, th*). (S)
I can decode one-syllable words by sounding out each letter. (S)
I can recognize long vowel sounds created using a final -e and common vowel teams. (K)
I can recognize that all syllables have a vowel sound. (K)
I can determine the number of syllables in a word by counting the vowel sounds. (S)
I can decode two syllable words by breaking them into vowel sound segments. (S)
I can identify words with common inflectional endings (e.g., *-s, -ed, -ing*) and read them correctly. (S)
I can recognize and read irregularly spelled words. (S)

Vocabulary

digraph, decode, syllable, vowel sound, vowel team, segment, inflectional ending, irregular

R

RF.1.3

Foundational Skills

CCR

(Not applicable to Foundational Skills)

Standard

Read with sufficient accuracy and fluency to support comprehension.

a. Read grade-level text with purpose and understanding.
b. Read grade-level text orally with accuracy, appropriate rate, and expression.
c. Use context to confirm or self-correct word recognition and understanding, rereading as necessary.

Enduring Understanding

Fluent readers accurately process print with expression at an appropriate rate.

Essential Questions

What do good readers do?
Why does fluency matter?

Suggested Learning Targets

I can explain that reading fluently means my reading is easy, smooth, and automatic. (K)
I can read grade-level text fluently and demonstrate my comprehension with meaningful voice, timing, and expression. (S)
I can recognize when a word I have read does not make sense. (S)
I can self-correct misread or misunderstood words using context clues. (S)
I can reread with corrections when necessary. (S)
I can read fluently. (S)

Vocabulary

fluent, voice, timing, expression, context clue

| Text Types and Purposes*

CCR

Write arguments to support claims in an analysis of substantive topics or texts, using valid reasoning and relevant and sufficient evidence.

Standard

Write opinion pieces in which they introduce the topic or name the book they are writing about, state an opinion, supply a reason for the opinion, and provide some sense of closure.

These broad types of writing include many subgenres. See Appendix A for definitions of key writing types.

Enduring Understanding	Essential Questions
Writing should be purposely focused, detailed, organized, and sequenced in a way that clearly communicates the ideas to the reader.	What do good writers do? What's my purpose and how do I develop it?

Suggested Learning Targets

I can identify my opinion on a topic or book. (S)
I can support my opinion with a reason. (S)
I can write an opinion piece with an introduction, opinion, supporting reason, and conclusion. (P)

Vocabulary

opinion, reason, conclusion

W   **W.1.1**

Writing

CCR

Write informative/explanatory texts to examine and convey complex ideas and information clearly and accurately through the effective selection, organization, and analysis of content.

Standard

Write informative/explanatory texts in which they name a topic, supply some facts about the topic, and provide some sense of closure.

*These broad types of writing include many subgenres. See Appendix A for definitions of key writing types.

Enduring Understanding

Writing should be purposely focused, detailed, organized, and sequenced in a way that clearly communicates the ideas to the reader.

Essential Questions

What do good writers do?
What's my purpose and how do I develop it?

Suggested Learning Targets

I can select a topic and identify facts to share. (S)
I can write an informative paper with a topic, facts, and an ending sentence. (P)

Vocabulary

topic, fact

Writing

CCR

Write narratives to develop real or imagined experiences or events using effective technique, well-chosen details, and well-structured event sequences.

Standard

Write narratives in which they recount two or more appropriately sequenced events, include some details regarding what happened, use temporal words to signal event order, and provide some sense of closure.

*These broad types of writing include many subgenres. See Appendix A for definitions of key writing types.

Enduring Understanding

Writing should be purposely focused, detailed, organized, and sequenced in a way that clearly communicates the ideas to the reader.

Essential Questions

What do good writers do?
What's my purpose and how do I
  develop it?

Suggested Learning Targets

I can place story events in the correct order. (R)
I can write a story with events placed in the correct order. (P)
I can use details to describe what happened in my story. (S)
I can use words (e.g., before, during, after) to show event order in my story. (S)
I can write an ending for my story that provides a sense of closure (ties up all loose
  ends and leaves the reader satisfied). (P)

Vocabulary

event, narrative, closure

W

W.1.3

Writing

CCR

Produce clear and coherent writing in which the development, organization, and style are appropriate to task, purpose, and audience.

Standard

(Begins in grade 3)

(Begins in grade 3)

Writing

CCR

Develop and strengthen writing as needed by planning, revising, editing, rewriting, or trying a new approach.

Standard

With guidance and support from adults, focus on a topic, respond to questions and suggestions from peers, and add details to strengthen writing as needed.

Enduring Understanding

Producing clear ideas as a writer involves selecting appropriate style and structure for an audience and is strengthened through revision and technology.

Essential Questions

Writing clearly: What makes a difference?
Final product: What does it take?

Suggested Learning Targets

I can write about a topic. (P)
I can answer questions about my writing. (R)
I can listen to ideas my teachers and peers have about my writing. (S)
I can add details that will help the reader understand my topic. (S)

Vocabulary

topic, detail

W

W.1.5

Writing

CCR

Use technology, including the Internet, to produce and publish writing and to interact and collaborate with others.

Standard

With guidance and support from adults, use a variety of digital tools to produce and publish writing, including in collaboration with peers.

Enduring Understanding

Producing clear ideas as a writer involves selecting appropriate style and structure for an audience and is strengthened through revision and technology.

Essential Questions

Writing clearly: What makes a difference?

Final product: What does it take?

Suggested Learning Targets

I can identify digital tools (e.g., Word, Publisher, PowerPoint) that will help me produce and publish my writing. (K)

I can use digital tools to produce and publish my writing. (S)

I can use digital tools to work with others. (S)

Vocabulary

digital tools, publish

W

W.1.6

Writing

CCR

Conduct short as well as more sustained research projects based on focused questions, demonstrating understanding of the subject under investigation.

Standard

Participate in shared research and writing projects (e.g., explore a number of "how-to" books on a given topic and use them to write a sequence of instructions).

Enduring Understanding

Effective research presents an answer to a question, demonstrates understanding of the inquiry, and properly cites information from multiple sources.

What do good researchers do?
"Cut and Paste:" What's the problem?

Suggested Learning Targets

I can define research and explain how research is different from other types of writing. (R)
I can research a topic with others. (S)
I can work with others to write about a research topic. (S)

Vocabulary

research, topic

W   W.1.7

Writing

CCR

Gather relevant information from multiple print and digital sources, assess the credibility and accuracy of each source, and integrate the information while avoiding plagiarism.

Standard

With guidance and support from adults, recall information from experiences or gather information from provided sources to answer a question.

Enduring Understanding

Effective research presents an answer to a question, demonstrates understanding of the inquiry, and properly cites information from multiple sources.

Essential Questions

What do good researchers do?
"Cut and Paste:" What's the problem?

Suggested Learning Targets

I can answer questions using information recalled or gathered. (S)

Vocabulary

recall, source

Writing

CCR

Draw evidence from literary or informational texts to support analysis, reflection, and research.

Standard

(Begins in grade 4)

(Begins in grade 4)

.

Writing

CCR

Write routinely over extended time frames (time for research, reflection, and revision) and shorter time frames (a single sitting or a day or two) for a range of tasks, purposes, and audiences.

Standard

(Begins in grade 3)

(Begins in grade 3)

Speaking and Listening

CCR

Prepare for and participate effectively in a range of conversations and collaborations with diverse partners, building on others' ideas and expressing their own clearly and persuasively.

Standard

Participate in collaborative conversations with diverse partners about *grade 1 topics and texts* with peers and adults in small and larger groups.

a. Follow agreed-upon rules for discussions (e.g., listening to others with care, speaking one at a time about the topics and texts under discussion).

b. Build on others' talk in conversations by responding to the comments of others through multiple exchanges.

c. Ask questions to clear up any confusion about the topics and texts under discussion.

Enduring Understanding

Comprehension is enhanced through a collaborative process of sharing and evaluating ideas.

Essential Questions

What makes collaboration meaningful? Making meaning from a variety of sources: What will help?

Suggested Learning Targets

I can identify and follow the agreed upon rules for discussion. (P)
I can listen to the comments of others and share my own ideas. (S)
I can ask questions when I do not understand. (S)

Vocabulary

discussion, idea

SL

SL.1.1

Speaking and Listening

CCR

Integrate and evaluate information presented in diverse media and formats, including visually, quantitatively, and orally.

Standard

Ask and answer questions about key details in a text read aloud or information presented orally or through other media.

Enduring Understanding

Comprehension is enhanced through a collaborative process of sharing and evaluating ideas.

Essential Questions

What makes collaboration meaningful? Making meaning from a variety of sources: What will help?

Suggested Learning Targets

I can identify information from a text being read aloud. (K)
I can identify information that is presented in different formats (e.g., media, charts, graphs, websites, speeches). (K)
I can ask and answer questions about key details in a text or presentation. (S)

Vocabulary

key detail, presentation

Speaking and Listening

CCR

Evaluate a speaker's point of view, reasoning, and use of evidence and rhetoric.

Standard

Ask and answer questions about what a speaker says in order to gather additional information or clarify something that is not understood.

Enduring Understanding

Comprehension is enhanced through a collaborative process of sharing and evaluating ideas.

Essential Questions

What makes collaboration meaningful? Making meaning from a variety of sources: What will help?

Suggested Learning Targets

I can ask questions about a presentation when I do not understand or need more information. (S)

I can answer questions about a speaker's presentation. (K)

Vocabulary

presentation

Speaking and Listening

CCR

Present information, findings, and supporting evidence such that listeners can follow the line of reasoning and the organization, development, and style are appropriate to task, purpose, and audience.

Standard

Describe people, places, things, and events with relevant details, expressing ideas and feelings clearly.

Enduring Understanding

Presentation of knowledge and ideas is enhanced through appropriate organization and style for an audience via the use of visual displays, technology, and the appropriate use of language.

Essential Questions

What makes a presentation "great"? "What I say" versus "how I say it", does it really matter?

Suggested Learning Targets

I can use details to describe people, places, things, and events. (S)
I can express ideas and feelings clearly. (S)

Vocabulary

detail, people, place, thing, event

SL

SL.1.4

Speaking and Listening

CCR

Make strategic use of digital media and visual displays of data to express information and enhance understanding of presentations.

Standard

Add drawings or other visual displays to descriptions when appropriate to clarify ideas, thoughts, and feelings.

Enduring Understanding

Presentation of knowledge and ideas is enhanced through appropriate organization and style for an audience via the use of visual displays, technology, and the appropriate use of language.

Essential Questions

What makes a presentation "great"? "What I say" versus "how I say it", does it really matter?

Suggested Learning Targets

I can identify places in my work where ideas, thoughts, or feelings are not clear. (S)
I can add drawings or visual displays (e.g., illustrations, graphs, photos) to clarify my ideas, thoughts, or feelings. (P)

Vocabulary

idea, thought, feeling, visual display, clarify

SL

SL.1.5

Speaking and Listening

CCR

Adapt speech to a variety of contexts and communicative tasks, demonstrating command of formal English when indicated or appropriate.

Standard

Produce complete sentences when appropriate to task and situation.

Enduring Understanding

Presentation of knowledge and ideas is enhanced through appropriate organization and style for an audience via the use of visual displays, technology, and the appropriate use of language.

Essential Questions

What makes a presentation "great"? "What I say" versus "how I say it", does it really matter?

Suggested Learning Targets

I can recognize a complete sentence (a group of words that expresses a complete thought). (K)
I can use complete sentences when needed. (S)

Vocabulary

complete sentence

SL

SL.1.6

Language

CCR

Demonstrate command of the conventions of standard English grammar and usage when writing or speaking.

Standard

Demonstrate command of the conventions of standard English grammar and usage when writing or speaking.

a. Print all upper- and lowercase letters.
b. Use common, proper, and possessive nouns.
c. Use singular and plural nouns with matching verbs in basic sentences (e.g., *He hops; We hop*).
d. Use personal, possessive, and indefinite pronouns (e.g., *I, me, my; they, them, their, anyone, everything*).
e. Use verbs to convey a sense of past, present, and future (e.g., *Yesterday I walked home; Today I walk home; Tomorrow I will walk home*).
f. Use frequently occurring adjectives.
g. Use frequently occurring conjunctions (e.g., *and, but, or, so, because*).
h. Use determiners (e.g., articles, demonstratives).
i. Use frequently occurring prepositions (e.g., *during, beyond, toward*).
j. Produce and expand complete simple and compound declarative, interrogative, imperative, and exclamatory sentences in response to prompts.

Enduring Understanding

Effective communication of ideas when speaking or writing relies on the appropriate use of the conventions of language.

Essential Questions

Why do the rules of language matter? Communicating clearly: What does it take?

Suggested Learning Targets

I can print all upper- and lowercase letters correctly. (S)

(continued on next page)

Vocabulary

uppercase letter, lowercase letter, common noun, proper noun, possessive noun, verb, singular, plural, pronoun, personal pronoun, possessive pronoun, indefinite pronoun conjunction, determiner, preposition, simple sentence, compound sentence

L

L.1.1

Language

CCR

Demonstrate command of the conventions of standard English grammar and usage when writing or speaking.

Standard

Demonstrate command of the conventions of standard English grammar and usage when writing or speaking.

a. Print all upper- and lowercase letters.
b. Use common, proper, and possessive nouns.
c. Use singular and plural nouns with matching verbs in basic sentences (e.g., *He hops; We hop*).
d. Use personal, possessive, and indefinite pronouns (e.g., *I, me, my; they, them, their, anyone, everything*).
e. Use verbs to convey a sense of past, present, and future (e.g., *Yesterday I walked home; Today I walk home; Tomorrow I will walk home*).
f. Use frequently occurring adjectives.
g. Use frequently occurring conjunctions (e.g., *and, but, or, so, because*).
h. Use determiners (e.g., articles, demonstratives).
i. Use frequently occurring prepositions (e.g., *during, beyond, toward*).
j. Produce and expand complete simple and compound declarative, interrogative, imperative, and exclamatory sentences in response to prompts.

Suggested Learning Targets

(continued from previous page)

I can explain the difference between common nouns (a general person, place, or thing), proper nouns (a specific person, place, or thing), and possessive nouns (a noun that shows ownership). (R)

I can identify and write common nouns correctly by beginning them with lowercase letter. (S)

I can identify and write proper nouns correctly by beginning them with capital letters. (S)

I can identify and write possessive nouns correctly by adding an apostrophe. (S)

I can write basic sentences that use singular nouns with singular verbs and plural nouns with plural verbs. (S)

(continued on next page)

Language

CCR

Demonstrate command of the conventions of standard English grammar and usage when writing or speaking.

Standard

Demonstrate command of the conventions of standard English grammar and usage when writing or speaking.

a. Print all upper- and lowercase letters.
b. Use common, proper, and possessive nouns.
c. Use singular and plural nouns with matching verbs in basic sentences (e.g., *He hops; We hop*).
d. Use personal, possessive, and indefinite pronouns (e.g., *I, me, my; they, them, their, anyone, everything*).
e. Use verbs to convey a sense of past, present, and future (e.g., *Yesterday I walked home; Today I walk home; Tomorrow I will walk home*).
f. Use frequently occurring adjectives.
g. Use frequently occurring conjunctions (e.g., *and, but, or, so, because*).
h. Use determiners (e.g., articles, demonstratives).
i. Use frequently occurring prepositions (e.g., *during, beyond, toward*).
j. Produce and expand complete simple and compound declarative, interrogative, imperative, and exclamatory sentences in response to prompts.

Suggested Learning Targets

(continued from previous page)

I can define pronoun (a word that takes the place of a noun or noun phrase). (K)
I can identify and use personal, possessive, and indefinite pronouns correctly. (S)
I can identify that verbs change when showing actions that happened in the past, present, or future and use verbs correctly. (S)
I can identify common conjunctions and use them correctly to combine words and phrases. (S)
I can explain that determiners are words that introduce nouns and use common determiners (e.g., *a, an, the, this, that, these*) and use them in my writing. (S)
I can identify common prepositions and use them correctly. (S)
I can respond to questions by writing simple and compound sentences. (S)
I can write simple and compound sentences that make a statement, ask a question, make a command/request, or make an exclamation. (S)

L

L.1.1 *(cont.)*

Language

CCR

Demonstrate command of the conventions of standard English capitalization, punctuation, and spelling when writing.

Standard

Demonstrate command of the conventions of standard English capitalization, punctuation, and spelling when writing.

a.   Capitalize dates and names of people.
b.   Use end punctuation for sentences.
c.   Use commas in dates and to separate single words in a series.
d.   Use conventional spelling for words with common spelling patterns and for frequently occurring irregular words.
e.   Spell untaught words phonetically, drawing on phonemic awareness and spelling conventions.

Enduring Understanding

Effective communication of ideas when speaking or writing relies on the appropriate use of the conventions of language.

Essential Questions

Why do the rules of language matter? Communicating clearly: What does it take?

Suggested Learning Targets

I can capitalize days of the week, months, and names of people when writing. (S)
I can identify end punctuation marks such as a period, exclamation point, and question mark. (K)
I can use the correct end punctuation in my writing. (S)
I can place a comma between the day and the year of a date. (S)
I can use a comma to separate three or more words in a series (e.g., *I went to the store to buy eggs, milk, and cheese.*). (S)
I can use common spelling patterns when writing words. (S)
I can spell new words by sounding out letters and using known spelling rules. (S)

Vocabulary

capitalize, period, exclamation point, question mark, punctuation, comma, series, spelling pattern

Language

CCR

Apply knowledge of language to understand how language functions in different contexts, to make effective choices for meaning or style, and to comprehend more fully when reading or listening.

Standard

(Begins in grade 2)

(Begins in grade 2)

Language

CCR

Determine or clarify the meaning of unknown and multiple-meaning words and phrases by using context clues, analyzing meaningful word parts, and consulting general and specialized reference materials, as appropriate.

Standard

Determine or clarify the meaning of unknown and multiple-meaning words and phrases based on *grade 1 reading and content*, choosing flexibly from an array of strategies.

a. Use sentence-level context as a clue to the meaning of a word or phrase.
b. Use frequently occurring affixes as a clue to the meaning of a word.
c. Identify frequently occurring root words (e.g., *look*) and their inflectional forms (e.g., *looks, looked, looking*).

Enduring Understanding

Effective readers and writers use knowledge of the structure and context of language to acquire, clarify, and appropriately use vocabulary.

Essential Questions

When a word doesn't make sense, what can I do?

How do I use what I know to figure out what I don't know?

Suggested Learning Targets

I can determine the meaning of unknown and multiple meaning words using context clues (e.g., definitions, examples, restatements) in a sentence. (R)

I can identify common affixes (e.g., *pre-, un-, -less*) of unknown words. (K)

I can use affixes to help me define new words. (S)

I can identify root words and understand that adding *-s, -ed*, and *-ing* changes the meaning of a root word. (K)

Vocabulary

context clue, affix, root word

L

L.1.4

Language

CCR

Demonstrate understanding of word relationships and nuances in word meanings.

Standard

With guidance and support from adults, demonstrate understanding of figurative language, word relationships and nuances in word meanings.

a. Sort words into categories (e.g., colors, clothing) to gain a sense of the concepts the categories represent.

b. Define words by category and by one or more key attributes (e.g., a *duck* is a bird that swims; a *tiger* is a large cat with stripes).

c. Identify real-life connections between words and their use (e.g., note places at home that are *cozy*).

d. Distinguish shades of meaning among verbs differing in manner (e.g., *look, peek, glance, stare, glare, scowl*) and adjectives differing in intensity (e.g., *large, gigantic*) by defining or choosing them or by acting out the meanings.

Enduring Understanding

Effective readers and writers use knowledge of the structure and context of language to acquire, clarify, and appropriately use vocabulary.

Essential Questions

When a word doesn't make sense, what can I do?

How do I use what I know to figure out what I don't know?

Suggested Learning Targets

I can sort words into categories. (S)

I can define words by categories using common traits. (S)

I can connect words I hear and read to the real world. (S)

I can tell the difference between similar verbs by defining, choosing, or acting out the meanings. (S)

I can tell the difference between similar adjectives by defining, choosing, or acting out the meanings. (S)

Vocabulary

common, category, trait, connection, verb, adjective

L   **L.1.5**

Language

CCR

Acquire and use accurately a range of general academic and domain-specific words and phrases sufficient for reading, writing, speaking, and listening at the college and career readiness level; demonstrate independence in gathering vocabulary knowledge when encountering an unknown term important to comprehension or expression.

Standard

Use words and phrases acquired through conversations, reading and being read to, and responding to texts, including using frequently occurring conjunctions to signal simple relationships (e.g., *because*).

Enduring Understanding

Effective readers and writers use knowledge of the structure and context of language to acquire, clarify, and appropriately use vocabulary.

Essential Questions

When a word doesn't make sense, what can I do?
How do I use what I know to figure out what I don't know?

Suggested Learning Targets

I can discover new words and phrases through reading, listening, and conversation. (S)
I can use my new words and phrases when speaking and writing. (S)
I can use conjunctions when speaking and writing. (S)

Vocabulary

list, phrase, conjunction